SOME SHORT
for the Sundays
Y

G000124426

# GLORIFYING
# THE LORD
# BY YOUR LIFE

# James O'Kane

## *Acknowledgment*

Use has been made throughout of the English version of Volume I of the Roman Lectionary approved for use in Ireland in 1981.

## The Homilist

Father James O'Kane was born in Belfast where he received his earliest education from Dominican Sisters and at Christian Brothers' schools. After seminary formation in Belfast and Rome he undertook postgraduate studies at Louvain and was ordained in 1976. From 1979 he taught spiritual and moral theology at Maynooth. Since 1995 he has served in Newtownards & Comber, Ballintoy & Ballinlea, Culfeightrin, Kilcoo and Cushendun & Torr.

## Second Sunday

*They have no wine*
.

A wedding without wine, brothers
and sisters in Christ, is a powerful
symbol of a life without joy. Jesus
was provoked by the failure of the
wine that day at that wedding at
Cana in Galilee. He was provoked
into giving the first of his signs. Not
just enough wine to keep the party
going but an enormous quantity and
the very best. He was provoked too
when he saw lives without joy,
provoked enough to die on the cross
so that men and women might learn
to die to self and be set free for lives
transfigured by joy. And not just
those first disciples. Not just the
people of his own time and place.
From the cross Jesus sends his Spirit
upon all the centuries to come. The
Spirit of Jesus is there for us, ready
at every moment to lift us out of the
dreariness of sin and set our lives

ablaze with the glory of God that alone brings joy and peace to the human heart. There is enough of the Spirit for everyone, today and for generations yet to come.

Why then do we all experience such an absence of joy, in our own lives and in the lives of those around us? It is not because the Spirit of God in not there. It is because we are so good at blocking the Spirit. We withhold our assent. We fail to collaborate. And it takes life's hardest knocks to teach us that the joy our soul thirsts for will always elude us for as long as we are busy with our own agenda. There will always be something missing for as long as we insist on going our own way. The Spirit of God summons us to community, togetherness, a sense of Church, belonging and sharing.

Saint Paul puts it magnificently, this business about the Spirit and the community it creates and the intoxication of it. There is a variety of gifts, he says, but always the same Spirit. There are all sorts of service to be done, but always to the same

Lord. Working in all sorts of different ways in different people, it is the same God who is working in all of them. Each of us has our own little place in the great plan. Joy comes when we open our hearts to the Spirit of God, when, letting go of everything else, we surrender at last to our own particular gift, the task of service that is ours alone.

Jesus is provoked every time he sees us living without joy. His disciples are not those with sad and gloomy faces. His disciples are those who have seen his glory in their own lives and believe in him with all their hearts. It is not true that we have no wine. We have kept the best wine to the last without knowing it. That discovery is the real and crowning joy of Christian discipleship.

*Isaiah 62:1-5 / First Corinthians 12:4-11 / John 2:1-11*

## *Third Sunday*

*This text is being fulfilled today even as you listen.*

Today, brothers and sisters in Christ, the Church begins the Sunday reading of the Gospel of Luke. Luke is the author of the third Gospel and of the Acts of the Apostles. He writes for someone called Theophilus - the name means 'Friend of God'. At this distance we cannot know whether Theophilus was a real individual person to whom Luke dedicated his accounts of Jesus and his disciples. What is certain is that Luke writes for all friends of God. He writes for us, in search of God, as we all are in our own way, in this our own time and place. 'Friend of God' is a happy term for it resonates in our conscience and in our conscience we know with clarity and immediacy whether being a 'Friend of God' is important to us or not.

Like us, Luke did not meet Jesus in the flesh. He came to faith, from a pagan background, through the preaching and friendship of the Apostle Paul. He writes to strengthen us in our conviction by offering us an ordered account of the testimony of those who were there, the eyewitnesses who reported and handed on what they had seen and heard for themselves, the whole story of Jesus from the beginning. In Jesus Luke discovers, for himself and for us, a God of mercy and compassion, a God concerned for the poor and the disadvantaged, a God concerned for the sick and the sinful, the sort of God the world needs, still needs today, and will always need, the God of the Good Samaritan, the God of the Father of the Prodigal Son.

The Sunday gospels for the rest of this Church year will take us through Luke's Gospel. It might be a good idea for us to take the trouble to find a copy of Luke's Gospel, written for the friends of God and for those in search of God, and read it from beginning to end for ourselves. A first reading needn't take much more than half an hour. And if you enjoy it you will be looking forward to the sequel, the Acts of the Apostles, the

11

working out of the Gospel of Jesus in the lives of his disciples, the building up of the body of Christ in the first Christian communities, the story the Church returns to every year in the fifty days of Easter.

Yes, we're sort of interested in Jesus but it might really be just too much trouble to go looking for a Gospel and trying to read it from beginning to end. In earlier times, before widespread literacy and before printing, people were glad to have something read to them, like the people in that extract from Nehemiah who were happy to stand from early morning until noon listening attentively as Ezra read to them from the Book of the Law and explained God's law to them. And indeed because they couldn't read themselves or didn't have access to the written text, they had no doubt better memories for what they heard read to them and were able to recall it, perhaps even word for word, when they needed it for daily living and the changing circumstances of their lives.

"The people of the Book" is an ancient expression that today might well be taken to embrace the whole family of Abraham - Jews, Christians and Moslems alike, those who believe in the one true God and seek to worship and glorify him by their lives. It is only in returning to the Book that we will come to know how far we have strayed and find the will to make a fresh start.

*Nehemiah 8:2-6.8-10 / First Corinthians 12:12-30 / Luke 1:1-4; 4:14-21*

## *Fourth Sunday*

*They sprang to their feet and hustled him out of the town.*

This was not, brothers and sisters in Christ, how it was meant to end. Or, at least, so we might think. Still, for Jesus himself, it was but a foretaste of the death that awaited him. The blandness of political correctness is so much safer than the naked truth, as we all learn sooner or later. And yet something wonderful does happen when our hearts are set free from all that distracts us from the truth, when we are - as Saint Paul invites us to be - ambitious for the higher gifts. Now we are seeing a dim reflection in a mirror; but then we shall be seeing face to face. The knowledge we have now is imperfect; but then we shall know as fully as we are known. Faith and hope and love.

Sometimes we do indeed catch glimpses of love, in our own lives, and in the lives of others. Or at least we hear stories of love that bring a tear to our eyes: Good Samaritans, fathers and mothers of prodigal sons and daughters, some gentle hint of God's love for us and his invitation to love one another on his behalf.

Love is always patient and kind. We are not always patient and kind. Love is not jealous. We sometimes are. Love is never boastful or conceited. It is never rude or selfish. We often have cause to regret what we have said or done. Love takes no pleasure in other people's sins. We frequently do. Love delights in the truth. Love is always ready to excuse, to trust, to hope, and to endure whatever comes.

Always this and never that. The always and never of this love challenge us about our compromises, our blind spots, our failures. Now we are seeing a dim reflection in a mirror but that dim reflection is the promise that then we shall be seeing face to face.

Love delights in the truth. So much of our experience of what passes for love is in the realm of fantasy and dream, an easy escape from reality.

Entering into truth is not always immediately delightful. It can be an all too painful process. But love delights in the truth. The first condition of love is to know ourselves and to see other people as they really are - not as we imagine them to be, and certainly not as we would like them to be for our own pleasure or convenience.

The first condition of love is reality. We have all, perhaps, had some experience of how blind a certain kind of love can be. Real love delights in the truth. It takes the trouble to see people as they really are in the freshness of the present moment. This is a beginning of freedom, a freedom that is the beginning of a real and genuine love, a selfless and sacrificial love.

The knowledge that I have now is imperfect, admits St Paul. But then I shall know as fully as I am known. It is unnerving to be loved without being known. It is devastating to be known and not loved. Jesus offers us something better: the fullness of truth and the fullness of love, gifts of his

Spirit that bring us a real joy and a real peace. Now indeed we are seeing a dim reflection in a mirror; but then we shall be seeing face to face. In the meantime, in our enraged frustration at the failure of our sins to bring us any of the satisfactions we think will make us happy, we will continue to hustle Jesus out of our lives - and he, wisely, will continue to slip through the crowd and walk away from us, until our time comes and the moment is right and we are ready to put our childish ways behind us.

*Jeremiah 1:4-5.17-19 / First Corinthians 12:31 – 13:13 / Luke 4:21-30*

## *Fifth Sunday*

*They left everything and followed him.*

It is our vocation, brothers and sisters in Christ, as disciples of Jesus, to become fully human and truly ourselves in the service of one another. And Jesus does offer his disciples a real possibility of fulfilling that vocation. For we do it by accepting the little place assigned to us in the great plan - and that acceptance involves us in the Christian mystery of death and resurrection: our death to what we would like to make of ourselves, our resurrection to the fullness of life that God is offering us.

The real test of a human being is not their success or failure in achieving what they have set out to achieve. The real test is how we fulfil the role that our destiny has assigned to us. It is difficult to know exactly what role has been assigned to us. We may never be told what it is in this life. It is not important for us to know. It can be very bad for us to be too sure that we do know. We have all seen people suffering from that delusion.

Simon Peter was to be the rock upon which Jesus would build his Church and yet it is unlikely that he died knowing that he was the first Pope. Indeed tradition suggests that his last thoughts were of his unworthiness to be a disciple of Jesus at all. That day by the lake, in the presence of Jesus, he felt his own sinfulness most keenly. Perhaps that was precisely why he and his companions left everything and followed Jesus. They cannot have been discontent with their lives in any ordinary sense. They were fishermen, which meant steady employment, the security and comfort of family life, the respect and support of their community. And yet, we are told, they left everything and followed him.

Jesus calls each one of us gathered here today. If that were not the case we would not bother to come to Mass. His call reminds us, if we need to be reminded, that our own attempts at being human have not perhaps been spectacularly successful. Our own attempts at love and service have left us hurt and wounded. For sin separates us from the divine in ourselves. Jesus offers healing, redemption, salvation.

Our first reaction to holiness is always to flee. With Simon Peter we say to Jesus: Leave me, Lord, for I am a sinner. But Jesus died to free us from sin. He does not easily give up on us. Indeed the subsequent story of Peter, his awkwardness, his betrayal, high-lights the patience and compassion that Jesus reserves for each one of us. Do not be afraid, he tells us. For, after all, it is fear that drives us to sin. Do not be afraid, he tells us as he offers us a better employment of our lives and talents and Christian discipleship leads us through death and resurrection to the highest fulfilment of our humanity.

Yes, Jesus calls us too to leave everything and follow him. And for most of us that means, paradoxically, staying exactly where we are and making the best of ourselves in the service of those who have been entrusted to us. It need not surprise us that staying where we are can require the longest of journeys and the most ruthless detachment.

*Isaiah 6:1-6 / First Corinthians 15:1-11 / Luke 5:1-11*

## **Sixth Sunday**

*The Lord guards the way of the just but the way of the wicked leads to doom.*

It is a good idea, brothers and sisters in Christ, for us to allow religion to challenge us now and again about what is important to us in life. Today's Scripture readings serve this purpose well. They remind us that we have a choice about how we live. They suggest that the better choice is not perhaps the obvious one. And St Paul cautions us that Christianity will always be a problematic option: if our hope in Christ has been for this life only, we are the most unfortunate of all people.

We have a choice. And our choice becomes apparent over the course of our lifetime. The Last Judgment is something of a formality. There is no talk of borderline cases or appeals to a higher court. But any judgment before death is premature. Where there's life there's hope of repentance and conversion - and the danger too of a final, devastating temptation and hardness of heart.

We have a choice. Sometimes we pause, especially at important moments in our lives, formally to put our choice into words, in the shape of resolutions and commitments. Or perhaps we think that we are postponing our choice. But that is always an illusion. Our choice is being made as the days and months and years vanish behind us. The present moment is never neutral. We stand at this very moment at a crossroads, poised to confirm the choice that we have already made - or about to undermine it. Everything we do, and the way we do it, affirms or rejects the choice that we have made thus far.

The Beatitudes of Jesus emphasize how peculiarly difficult the choice before us is. Happy the poor, happy the hungry, happy those who weep now. Alas for the rich, alas for those who have their fill, alas for those who laugh now. If Jesus is to be trusted then our choice is obvious. But Paul does not camouflage the risk we take: If our hope in Christ has been for this life only, we are the most unfortunate of all people. Our choice vacillates as our focus shifts between present pleasure and future happiness. The temptation to make ourselves comfortable in the present is very urgent and makes perfect sense if death is the end. It is the way of the world and has been since the beginning.

The religious view is based on the certainty that present pleasure and present pain will become dim memories as the future, whatever it is, becomes our permanent reality, The promise of Jesus is that those who are poor now will be rich then in a way that the rich never were; that those who hunger now will be satisfied then in a way never imagined by the self-indulgent; that those who weep now will laugh then with a divine laughter unknown to the shallow comedians of this world.

The choice is at every moment entirely our own. It helps to admit that it is a difficult choice, an awesome responsibility.

## Sundays in Ordinary Time – Year C

*Jeremiah 17:5-8 / First Corinthians 15:12.16-20 / Luke 6:17.20-26*

## Seventh Sunday

*The first man, Adam, as scripture says, became a living soul. But the last Adam has become a life-giving spirit.*

We struggle, brothers and sisters in Christ, in our first contacts with the human world, to become a living soul and then, in our encounters with the life-giving spirit we find in Jesus, very much to our surprise, we are offered the gift of becoming ourselves a life-giving spirit for others. As we establish ourselves on earth the hope of heaven is held out to us, a definitive fulfilment well beyond our legitimate expectations. Successfully modelled on the earthly man we can go on to be modelled on the heavenly man.

The Gospel words of Jesus tempt us beyond such goodness as comes naturally to us as human beings. If you do good only to those who do good to you, what thanks can you expect? I say this to you who are listening: Love your enemies, do good to those who hate you, bless those who curse you, pray for those who treat you badly.

But perhaps we are not really listening. Or perhaps despite our best listening we fail really to hear what is being said, this urgent push to go beyond the merely human. Perhaps indeed to merely human ears the words of Jesus seem too absurd to be taken seriously. Treat others as you would like them to treat you. Well, yes. That does express a certain good sense, a certain moral maturity even. But turning the other cheek? Inviting the thief to keep what he has stolen from you? And even offering him something more? Not insisting on your rights?

No, doing the Christian thing, as we might call it, has little to recommend it in human terms. It is just too much. It makes no sense. At the very least we would look foolish.

Doing the Christian thing. We do not easily grasp that Jesus wants to drag us into a different dimension where we are promised a great reward, the assurance that we are children of a God of whose essence it is to be kind to the ungrateful and the wicked.

Be compassionate as your Father is compassionate, whispers Jesus. Do not judge, and you will not be judged yourselves. Do not condemn and you will not be condemned yourselves. Grant pardon, and you will be pardoned.

Jesus became a living soul in the best of our human world so that he might be to us a life-giving spirit transforming us too into life-giving spirits to others. We who have been modelled on the earthly man, will be modelled on the heavenly man.

Compassion is the key to this transformation. It is totally contagious. The amount you measure out is the amount you will be given back.

*First Samuel 26:2.7-9.12-13.22-23 / First Corinthians 15:45-49 / Luke 6:27-38*

## *Eighth Sunday*

*In a shaken sieve the rubbish is left behind.... Do not praise a man before he has spoken....*

Jesus discourages us from judging others, brothers and sisters in Christ. He discourages us specifically from judging one another – and in the strongest possible terms. And yet wherever two or three are gathered together no opportunity is missed to assess and diminish someone who is not there. Wherever two or three are gathered together a cheerful character assassination is often in progress.

Do not praise a man before he has spoken, the defects of a man appear in his talk. In a shaken sieve the rubbish is left behind.

Jesus suggests that it is not ultimately in our own best interests to misuse the gift of speech in this way. Do not judge and you will not be judged yourselves. What reward could be more attractive? Yet again and again we let ourselves go and, before we know it, we have said too much.

Can one blind man guide another? Surely both will fall into a pit. Why is it that we always know what is best for others but are often rather slow to take our own advice? Why do we so confidently diagnose the splinter in our brother's eye and never think to deal with the great plank in our own?

The failure of the disciples of Jesus to take these hints of his explains at least why we have made so little progress over the years of our own lives and over the many generations of Christian history.

Is it likely, is it possible that change will come any time soon? Hypocrite! Take the plank out of your own eye first and then you will see clearly enough to take out the splinter that is in your brother's eye.

We need to pull down all the massive screens behind which we have hidden, and hidden chiefly from ourselves, and so face the naked truth which alone can set us free. We are offered in Jesus the grace of beginning afresh every morning, beginning afresh with ourselves and with our own conversion.

Never give in then, my dear brothers and sisters, St Paul encourages us. Never admit defeat. Keep on working at the Lord's work always. Know that, in the Lord, you cannot be working in vain.

In a shaken sieve the rubbish is left behind. And good riddance to it.

*Ecclesiasticus 27:4-7 / First Corinthians 15:54-58 / Luke 6:39-45*

## *Tenth Sunday*

*O Lord, you have raised my soul from the dead, restored me to life from those who sink into the grave.*

The resurrection of Jesus, brothers and sisters in Christ, is very different from this mere coming back to life of the son of Elijah's landlady or the son of the widow at Nain. The resurrection of Jesus is very different because it marks the beginning of a new quality of life for him, a life that will last forever, a life that will be shared with all those who believe in him. We might well wonder about the point of bringing someone back to life when they will only have to face death a second time. Indeed there is no suggestion that any favour is being done to either of these two young men. In both cases it is clearly for the sake of their widowed mothers that each of them is restored to life.

Many of us do in fact get a second chance at life, some of us even a third or fourth chance. We survive accidents or illnesses that might have killed us and nearly did. Are we now living better, fuller lives because of that experience or does the gift of extra time, a second chance, mean nothing to us. People dear to us have been restored to us when we were sure we had lost them. Do we now see them as a special gift or are we just as indifferent as ever? Sometimes it is perhaps easier for us to love someone when they are dead: we can remember them and mourn them the way we always wanted them to be now that they can no longer contradict us, now that they can no longer spoil our fantasy by merely being themselves in the freedom and uncertainty of their future.

Surely it is even more tragic when a mother or father loses a child, not to death, but to misunderstanding or betrayal: a chasm opens up between them that can never be bridged by any human initiative. That miracle, the miracle of giving back lost sons and daughters to their estranged mothers and fathers, would be a miracle worthy of Jesus, the miracle of healing broken relationships, the miracle of reconciling enemies: such miracles are possible in the risen Lord, Jesus who has conquered death and now lives for ever. Such miracles are possible for the disciples of Jesus if only we would once and for all make our own the prayer he prescribed for us: Father, forgive us our trespasses as we forgive those who trespass against us. Lead us not into temptation but deliver us from evil.

For when we make the Lord's Prayer, the Our Father, our own, miracles happen and a new world begins: The Lord listened and had pity. The Lord came to my help. For me you have changed my mourning into dancing; O Lord my God, I will thank you for ever. I will praise you, Lord, you have rescued me and have not let my enemies rejoice over me. O Lord, you have raised my soul from the dead, restored me to life from those who sink into the grave. Amen.

*First Kings 17:17-24 / Galatians 1:11-19 / Luke 7:11-17*

## *Eleventh Sunday*

*But now I have acknowledged my sins; my guilt I did not hide. I said: I will confess my offence to the Lord. And you, Lord, have forgiven the guilt of my sin.*

Prostitution, brothers and sisters in Christ, in its broader sense, is when we sacrifice our human dignity, our personal truth, for some trivial, transient advantage. We forget those words of Jesus that we have perhaps not fully understood: what profit is it for you to gain the whole world at the cost of damaging your own soul? No doubt, looking back, we find the excuse that we were driven to it, whatever it was, but the fact of the matter is that we all have our price and we sometimes sell ourselves for very little.

This general pattern of human waywardness reveals itself to us more readily in the gossip-worthy behaviour of others than in any screams from our own conscience. Take King David in today's reading from the Old Testament. He seems to have been oblivious almost to the point of innocence to the outrageousness of his behaviour towards his neighbours Bathsheba and Uriah. One lazy afternoon strolling on his roof, when his men were all away at war, he spotted Bathsheba bathing at her house and, although he already had wives enough of his own, he sent for her. Some time later, when she had sent him word that she was pregnant, he summoned Uriah back from the front and, after a few polite enquiries about the war, he told him to go and spend a few days at home. A decent man, revolted at the suggestion of such a disloyalty to his comrades suffering at the front, Uriah refused this unexpected offer of home comforts. So David sent him back to the war with a letter for the General: Put Uriah in the front line, it said.

And so it was that King David found the prophet Nathan on his doorstep. Nathan told him about a rich sheep farmer with enormous flocks who, to feed an unexpected visitor, had taken and slaughtered the pet lamb of a poor neighbour. David was filled with righteous indignation: who was this man? what he wouldn't have done to him. But Nathan said to him: You are that man. And at last it dawned on David: I have sinned against the Lord. Or as we find the experience detailed in the words of today's Psalm: Now I have acknowledged my sins; my guilt I did not hide. I said: I will confess my offence to the Lord. And you, Lord, have forgiven the guilt of my sin.

Sin and acknowledgment of sin. Confession and forgiveness. As disciples of Jesus we have access to a deeper insight into the dynamics of sin and forgiveness. For Jesus is not just another prophet, not just another witness to God's truth. Jesus has power over sin. Jesus can forgive sin. He approaches sinners with an extraordinary gentleness and compassion, the very revelation of the love and mercy of God himself. Indeed that is why Jesus has come into the world and why he will die on the cross and rise from the dead. Simon the Pharisee was unnerved by what was happening in his house: If this man were a prophet, he would know who this woman is that is touching him and what a bad name she has. He did not immediately realise that Jesus also knew exactly whose house he was eating in and why. For Jesus offers the divine forgiveness to us all. He longs to say to each one of us: Your faith has saved you. Go in peace.

Reading this Gospel story again we might notice that there is more than one prostitute in it. Reading this Gospel story again we might be struck by that chilling sentence: It is the man who is forgiven little who shows little love.

*Second Samuel 12:7-10.13 / Galatians 2:16.19-21 / Luke 7:36 – 8:3*

## *Twelfth Sunday*

*Anyone who wants to save his life will lose it.*

An old Chinese proverb, brothers and sisters in Christ, tells us that those who spend their time looking at themselves never shine. It is the message of Jesus too that it is in our self-forgetfulness that the glory of God shines through us bringing healing and peace to others. Too often we fail in life by trying too hard and we learn nothing from our failure. Anyone who wants to save their life, says Jesus, will lose it. It is a crushing thought, a terrible threat. How can we not want to save our lives? What are we to do when the very attempt itself means certain failure?

There are many ordinary experiences that teach us the wisdom of self-forgetfulness. Riding a bicycle or playing an instrument, speaking or singing, swimming or walking a tight-rope, even just walking or standing - it doesn't do to think too

39

much about what we are doing or we start to falter, we become anxious and fail. The secret is to let go, to stop watching ourselves, to relax into what we are doing. Our success depends on it, our safety and sometimes even our lives.

Why is it so difficult for us to apply this same wisdom to life itself? Why are we so self-preoccupied when the cost to ourselves and our personal truth is so great? Anyone who wants to save his life will lose it. Nothing is more certain. The very attempt guarantees failure. Those who spend their time looking at themselves never shine. Jesus makes us this promise: Anyone who loses their life for my sake, that person will save it. In Baptism the Christian plunges into death in the sure and certain hope of resurrection to new life. But our Baptism is not an once and for all event with no looking back. Our temptation is in fact to look back and we must not do that for when we do we lose the balance that is ours in Christ and we fall. Our Baptism is a permanent commitment that needs to be renewed and re-lived every day, at every hour of every day. If anyone wants to be a follower of mine, insists Jesus, let him renounce himself and take up his cross every day and follow me.

Yes, Jesus has promised us: Anyone who loses their life for my sake, that person will save it. If we can believe with Peter that Jesus is the Christ of God, if we can take the risk of faith, if we can desire with all our heart and soul to be his disciples, then let us by all means follow him. It involves first of all a decision about our past in which we plunge into the death of Baptism and renounce ourselves with vigour and determination. Only then we can begin to take up our cross every day and follow Jesus.

The gate is narrow, he said, and the way is hard, that leads to life, and those who find it are few. Enter by the narrow gate, he implores us, for the gate is wide and the way is easy, that leads to destruction, and those who enter by it are many. There is no escape from the cross. The truth, the unpleasant truth, is that those who fail to take up their cross and follow Jesus will be crucified anyway.

There is no escape from the cross. Down through the centuries Christians have meditated on the death of Jesus on the cross. And until the end of time they will continue to stand or kneel or sit in prayer before the crucifix until silent wisdom and inner peace overwhelm them and they come to know that they are loved. And in abandoning themselves to that love they forget themselves and begin to shine with the eternal brightness of the glory of God. By his passion and cross may we too be brought to the glory of his resurrection. Through Christ our Lord. Amen.

*Zechariah 12:10-11; 13:1 / Galatians 3:26-29 / Luke 9:18-24*

## *Thirteenth Sunday*

*If you are guided by the Spirit you will be in no danger of yielding to self-indulgence.*

If we find ourselves yielding to self-indulgence, brothers and sisters in Christ, it is a clear sign that we are not allowing ourselves to be guided by the Spirit. The trouble is that we rarely notice just how self-indulgent we actually are. At least not before it is too late. The unkind word has been spoken, the mean deed has been done. A confidence has been betrayed, a reputation destroyed. Health has been undermined, a family ruined. Yes, we all have our own personal list, our own personal experiences. And, of course, it is always so much easier to notice the harmful effects of someone else's self-indulgence. But in the end life confronts us with the consequences of our own.

It is often too late to avoid these consequences. What has been done cannot be undone. An opportunity that has been missed rarely returns. If you are guided by the Spirit you will be in no danger of yielding to self-indulgence - the words of Saint Paul cut across our self-pity and remind us that there is an alternative. We are not obliged to live lives of self-indulgence. The door of our prison is open. Our chains may be heavy but they are not securely fastened. We are called to freedom.

Christian freedom is a curious concept. It is quite different from the freedom the world aspires to, the untrammelled pursuit of pleasure and ambition which often ends so pitifully in the avoidance of pain and a frenzied attempt to control a shrinking environment. We mishear the message of Christ and find in the freedom he offers us only a new opening for self-indulgence. We seek in our religion the very security and success we are invited to surrender for the sake of our freedom in Christ, that true freedom which enables us to serve one another in works of love. If you go snapping at each other and tearing each other to pieces - yes, the ultimate self-indulgence and all too familiar.

It is an either-or situation. Self-indulgence is the opposite of the Spirit. It is precisely because the two are so opposed that we do not always carry out our good intentions. We would like to be good, sometimes. We would like to do the right thing, sometimes. We would like to be kind and even generous, sometimes. But it does not work like that. The Spirit is not there for us to use just whenever it suits us. It is in our willingness to be open to the Spirit of God in all things that we receive our freedom.

If we offer to follow Jesus in the hope of some sort of religious comfort or emotional security he reminds us: Foxes have holes and the birds of the air have nests, but the Son of Man has nowhere to lay his head. When we submit to sentiment and convention he shocks us beyond measure: Leave the dead to bury their dead. Your duty is to go and spread the news of the kingdom of God.

And when we ask to be his disciples on our own terms he tells us sternly: Once the hand is laid on the plough, no one who looks back is fit for the kingdom of God. Yes, when Christ freed us, he meant us to remain free. We are exhorted to stand firm and refuse to submit again to the yoke of slavery. It could be that we have abused religion as an opening for self-indulgence, some sort of promise of comfort and security in an uncertain world, even a guarantee of something or other in a life to come. It could be that we have missed the true excitement of our Christian calling and not yet tasted our freedom at all.

*First Kings 19:16.19-21 / Galatians 5:1.13-18 / Luke 9:51-62*

# *Fourteenth Sunday*

*The kingdom of God is very near you.*

The kingdom of God is very near you, brothers and sisters in Christ. This is the message the disciples of Jesus offer the human race as they pass through this world on their way to heaven. Inevitably it produces a variety of results, occasionally indeed a positive response, but all too often a negative and even hostile reaction. The disciples are not to bother themselves one way or the other. They are to keep going for they have a long way to go and they must not delay over the distractions of success or failure. It is the message that counts, and its urgency. The kingdom of God is very near to you. Be sure of this, the kingdom of God is very near.

We are all called, in our own way, in the circumstances of our lives, to add our own small voice to this chorus of witness. Sometimes the preacher, for example, expresses it in just the right way for someone and the voice of God is heard in a human heart.

Among those who hear the message some will remember that they have heard it before and what it meant to them then and be reassured and refreshed by that remembering. Others may really hear it for the very first time, and go home filled with new joy, new courage, new hope. Others will hear something and be angered, irritated, annoyed. And that too can be part of a spiritual journey, preparation for a fresh conversion. Many, it is true, never hear anything at all.

The kingdom of God is very near to you. The words of the preacher are, of course, nothing at all compared to the message conveyed by the sometimes very silent lives of genuine disciples. Be sure of this, they proclaim in their own quiet way, the kingdom of God is very near. For they are God's presence in our world, living witnesses to a genuinely alternative life-style, the eternal novelty of honesty, decency and service to others. This is the message of the disciples of Jesus to the time and place entrusted to them.

As we deliver this message, to the extent that we do, we begin to make it fully our own, in our hearts and in our lives. What matters, as Saint Paul puts it, is for us to become altogether new people, through the cross of our Lord Jesus Christ. The cross is the hidden strength of the Christian life. For Jesus our Saviour has shown us that the cross is the one way to win peace, mercy and grace for ourselves and for all who inhabit our world. If, like Paul and all God's saints, we bear the marks of Jesus on our lives, we are unavoidably and uncomfortably different. It is the only thing we can boast about, it is the only thing we should want to boast about, as we rejoice that our names too are written in heaven.

*Isaiah 66:10-14 / Galatians 6:14-18 / Luke 10:1-12.17-20*

## *Fifteenth Sunday*

*You must love the Lord your God with all your heart, with all your soul, with all your strength, and with all your mind, and your neighbour as yourself. You have answered right, said Jesus, do this and life is yours.*

The parable of the Good Samaritan that is read to us on this Sunday, brothers and sisters in Christ, arose out of the question about eternal life: Master, what must I do to inherit eternal life? I think we would all like to be Good Samaritans, even independently of eternal life. It is an attractive thing in itself. And yet it is so often our experience that we do in fact pass by on the other side - so often indeed that we begin to have some sympathy for the plight of the priest and the Levite in the parable. After all they were only doing what most of us do most of the time. It is the most natural thing in the world to pass by on the other side. Stopping to help someone can give rise to all kinds of complications and most of us don't much like complications. The Samaritan too did what came naturally to him. He was simply the sort of person who does that sort of thing. Jesus however commends his behaviour to us: Go, and do the same yourself. And the contrast is not lost on us. Samaritans, we sense, were not people you would expect much of. The priest and the Levite, on the other hand, were decent people, respectable people, religious people, people too much like ourselves perhaps. It must surely trouble us a little that they were the ones who passed by on the other side.

Love is the test of our sincerity. Not a forced love for there is no such thing, but a love that is genuine, a love that naturally does what is right. We have been called out of nothingness into being by the Creator-God who is our Father. We are called, again and again, out of the darkness of sin into the light of grace by Jesus, our Saviour-God who has come into our world to rescue and redeem us. We are called, ultimately, out of death into life by the Holy Spirit of God, giver of life and of love.

The proof that we have definitively passed out of death into life is that we do in fact actively love our brothers and sisters, our neighbours. It is not because we have loved that we merit eternal life. It is the other way round: it is because we have received the gift of eternal life that we are enabled to love. Jesus has shown us the way and not just in parables. He is himself the Good Samaritan who comes to meet us in the confusion of our lives, to rescue us from the brokenness of sin, to bind up our wounds, to get us back on our feet and launch us afresh along the right path that alone leads to life. His lesson in love is the cross, the gift of his life for us inviting us too to give all that we have and are for the good of our brothers and sisters, our neighbours.

Go and do the same yourself, Jesus tells us, for whatever you do to the least of your neighbours, my brothers and sisters, you do to me. And who is my neighbour? My neighbour is that person who in this present moment has most genuine need of my attention, my time, my resources.

It is as simple and as awesome as that, the path of love that leads inexorably to eternal life.

*Deuteronomy 30:10-14 / Colossians 1:15-20 / Luke 10:25-37*

## Sixteenth Sunday

*The mystery is Christ among you, your hope of glory.*

Martha, brothers and sisters in Christ, is too busy looking after Jesus to listen to him. It is a classic avoidance strategy and we all have our own versions of it. Christ is among us, our hope of glory and we have devised the nicest possible ways of avoiding him.

This story about Martha and Mary and their different ways of responding to the presence of Jesus in their home raises the question about the relationship between life and prayer, the relationship between serving Jesus in one another in everyday life and listening to Jesus in the stillness of our own hearts. Why is Martha wrong and Mary right? And what does it mean for us as we try to get it right in our own lives?

It is a question of balance and priority. Martha has started in the wrong place and her activity, however well-meant and good and practical in itself, is an expression of her restless anxiety. We need not doubt that Jesus did honour to the meal that Martha prepared for him but neither does he disguise his disappointment that her frenzied activity deprives him of the attention of her heart. It would have been a happier meal if she had allowed Jesus to take from her that restless anxiety that so quickly explodes in her angry complaint: Lord, do you not care that my sister is leaving me to the serving all by myself? Please tell her to help me. But Jesus does not care at all about that. He cares about something much more important: Martha, Martha, you worry and fret about so many things, and yet few are needed, indeed only one. It is Mary who has chosen the better part and it is not to be taken from her.

The better part, the one thing necessary. How are we to choose it and what would it mean for us? The advantage of Martha's sister is that she has started in the right place. She sat down at the Lord's feet and listened to him speaking. What she does when she has finished listening she will do differently. And that is perhaps the simplest lesson of all this, the reminder that it is not the quantity of what we do that counts but rather the quality of our actions. Martha's greatest pain will be the discovery, perhaps too late, that a humble meal prepared by the gentle serenity of a Mary is more pleasing than even the most sumptuous banquet produced by the distracted restlessness of her own fretful anxiety. The message of Jesus is that what we do is never as important as who we are. Nothing that we do, no matter what advantage it may bring to others, will ever compensate for what we ourselves are not.

If we find in our own hyperactivity the restless anxiety of a Martha trying to make up for what we are not, it is time for us to choose the better part, the one thing necessary. A sprinkling of prayer to season our days will give our lives a richer taste and awaken us to the presence of Christ in us and among us, our hope of glory.

*Sundays in Ordinary Time – Year C*

*Genesis 18:1-10 / Colossians 1:24-28 / Luke 10:38-42*

## *Seventeenth Sunday*

*Lord, teach us to pray.*

We are already praying, brothers and sisters in Christ, when we make this request. Lord, teach us to pray. Jesus gives us the Our Father, the Lord's Prayer and reminds us that true prayer is unending perseverance and absolute confidence in God.

Say this when you pray: Father, may your name be held holy, your kingdom come; give us each day our daily bread, and forgive us our sins, for we ourselves forgive each one who is in debt to us. And do not put us to the test.

It is of course Matthew's version that we know by heart. Luke's version always strikes us with a certain freshness and jolts us into a sense of how thoughtless our rushed recitation of the Lord's Prayer so often is. When we listen to what we are saying in the Our Father it becomes a potent examination of conscience. That is why we say it together as we prepare to receive Holy Communion.

Does the way I live my life allow me to say the Our Father without hypocrisy? Can I dare to call God my Father when I lack sincerity in my relation-ships with my brothers and sisters who are also called to be his children? May your name be held holy, your kingdom come. Can I really mean that when my whole life is such an effort to make a name for myself and build a little kingdom of my own?

Give us each day our daily bread. Can we really be content with so little? Are we not always praying for jam on our bread and more for tomorrow and next week and far beyond? Forgive us our sins, for we ourselves forgive each one who is in debt to us. But do we really want to take the risk of making these words our own? How can such a bargain be to our advantage when we are so slow to seek reconciliation with one another? So many of us have people we consider beyond the range of our forgiveness. How can we ask God to be no more merciful to us than we are to them? And do not put us to the test. A laughable prayer when we think how often we rush into all kinds of temptations of our own making.

Lord, teach us to pray. We are already praying. And it is only by praying that we learn to pray. Ask, and it will be given to you; search, and you will find; knock, and the door will be opened to you. For the one who asks always receives - perhaps not exactly what we ask for, but something rather better, all that we truly need. The one who searches always finds - though in truth we will never know what we are really looking for until we have found it. The one who knocks will always have the door opened to him - for we will notice in the end that it is on our side that the door is bolted.

Prayer works miracles. But perhaps we are too ready to shout miracle when we think we see God doing our will. The real miracle, the real answer to prayer, the real gift of the Holy Spirit, is when we find ourselves doing his will. May we learn to pray for that miracle, the only one that really matters.

*Sundays in Ordinary Time – Year C*

*Genesis 18:20-32 / Colossians 2:12-14 /
Luke 11:1-13*

# Eighteenth Sunday

*Vanity of vanities. All is vanity.*

Vanity, brothers and sisters in Christ, is a silliness we recognize more easily in the lives of others than in our own. The vain amuse us because they take it for granted that what they see in their mirror is exactly what the rest of us see and admire. Still, we all live with a certain level of personal vanity. At best it humbles us and teaches us to laugh at ourselves - a minor spiritual triumph in itself.

But the Old Testament Preacher is not much concerned with our little foibles and trifling compromises. His message is more radical and more strident. Vanity of vanities, he cries. Vanity of vanities. All is vanity. The whole thing, he insists, is utterly, utterly futile. Even the man who has laboured wisely, skilfully and successfully is called into question. What does it all come to in the end, his laborious days, his cares of office, his restless nights? Nothing, and less than nothing. Fool, this very night the demand will be made for your soul. And this hoard of yours, whose will it be then?

Jesus makes two comments on all this. Firstly on the general temptation to ask for more: Watch and be on your guard against avarice of any kind, he warns us, for your life is not made secure by what you own, even when you have more than you need. And secondly in response to the fate of the rich fool: This is the way it is when you store up treasure for yourself instead of making yourself rich in the sight of God. So we are warned about avarice: greed, as Colossians puts it, is the same thing as worshipping a false god. And we are left wondering what it might mean to make ourselves rich in the sight of God.

The story of the rich fool, of course, turns on death: This very night the demand will be made for your soul. But if we merely pity the rich fool his untimely death, and that is perhaps our initial reaction, we look rather like him and risk misunderstanding the real horror of his situation. The real horror is not that he is dead, and dead just at that moment when, as we might be tempted to put it in our worldly way, he had everything to look forward to. All is vanity and the real tragedy is that he has missed the point of life.

Yes, we are called to make ourselves rich in the sight of God and instead, driven by our fear of not having enough, we squander our lives in greed and avarice storing up treasure for ourselves. Fool! This very night the demand will be made for your soul. But what soul? The sadness of such a life is that it is soulless, futile, vain. It is the sadness of missing the whole point of life and losing one's soul.

Life is about something else altogether. The point of life is to become rich in the sight of God.

*Ecclesiastes 1:2; 2:21-23 / Colossians 3:1-5.9-11 / Luke 12:13-21*

## *Nineteenth Sunday*

*Happy those servants whom the master finds awake when he comes.*

It is impossible, brothers and sisters in Christ, to exaggerate the importance of the present moment. There is much to be said for remembering and celebrating our past. And it is generally prudent to plan for the future. But there is a real danger that we are only too willing to be distracted from the daunting reality of the present moment. Life is now. We postpone it at our peril. If we find ourselves too often killing time, as we say, we are, in fact, wasting our lives, dispersing our soul, squandering our very self.

My master is taking his time coming. It is perhaps a natural reaction after twenty centuries of Christian waiting for the Lord's return but it cannot be an excuse for us not to begin our Christian life, now, today. The master will come on a day we do not expect and at an hour we do not know. Happy those servants whom the master finds awake when he comes. Our temptation is to take our chance, to think that we can live any how and still manage to be awake at the right moment. Perhaps we have had experiences that have taught us that that just does not work. We have often enough been caught napping and missed opportunities that will never return. Of course we could learn from our mistakes, but that too we postpone. Tomorrow will be time enough, we think. But that is one tomorrow that never comes.

Life is now. We postpone it at our peril. The daunting reality of the present moment is the place where our destiny is being decided. And being awake in the present moment is not a cheap grace. It is the reward of a long practice. When we are young, and for as long as we still think of ourselves as young, our temptation is to live in the future. We look forward to what will never come and we waste our time in waiting. We slumber on, clinging to our fantasies, never awake to the reality that life is now, in the present moment, or not at all. Then, as we get older, and our future inexorably becomes our past, we make our home in that past clinging desperately to our illusions. The seeming advantage of such living in the past like that is that we avoid the present moment with all its challenge and possible pain. But we are asleep, and we risk dying in our sleep.

Awake, O sleeper, and arise from the dead, and Christ will give you light. Life is now or not at all. Jesus invites us to take the risk of waking up. There is no need to be afraid, little flock, he tells us, for it has pleased your Father to give you the kingdom. We do not have to wait. Life is now. The kingdom is now. Where your treasure is, Jesus reminds us, there will your heart be also. We can seek our treasure in the future and lose our heart in fantasy. We can bury our treasure in the past and wait for our heart to break. Jesus offers us the only way out: he invites us to accept the treasure of the present moment and live it, with all our heart, in the presence of God.

*Wisdom 18:6-9 / Hebrews 11:1-2.8-19 / Luke 12:32-48*

## *Twentieth Sunday*

*I have come to bring fire to the earth, and how I wish it were blazing already.*

Peace, brothers and sisters in Christ, is what we are promised at the end. We are not to expect an easy time along the way. As Jeremiah sank into the mud at the bottom of the well he will have taken some satisfaction in knowing that he had spoken as he had been given to speak and that he was paying the price of his unwelcome witness - or at least that is the spin he will have put on it in calm reflection after his rescue.

Unwelcome witness provokes hostility. There are, of course, those who positively revel in the hostility they provoke by their witness but most of us prefer to avoid it. Let's face it: we find witness embarrassing.

The death of Jesus on the cross marks a kind of culmination of the consistent response to unwelcome witness throughout history. His words and actions, his way of speaking about God, his way of reaching out to the people he encountered, were all too much of a challenge, too much of a threat, to the accepted ways of his time and place. He was too subversive. What would happen if everyone did the same? Unthinkable. He had to be stopped. And as his execution became inevitable his friends betrayed him and his disciples ran away.

But we have come to believe that the death of Jesus on the cross brings salvation and life for the whole world. We believe that Jesus rose from the dead, his witness accepted and confirmed by God. And we believe that we are called to be his witnesses in the various worlds we inhabit. For we have been baptised into his death in the hope of sharing his resurrection - already now in our daily lives and for all eternity in the glory of God.

Often, as we rise to the challenge of witness, we feel isolated and alone, like Jesus himself in the darkness of Gethsemane. But as the Letter to the Hebrews today encourages us: With so many witnesses in a great cloud on every side of us, we should throw off everything that hinders us, especially the sin that clings so easily, and keep running steadily in the race we have started.

The sin that clings so easily.... Sometimes our sin fits us so well that we hardly notice it. It fits us like a glove, like a second skin. Others speak of it as our character, the way we are, and they love or hate us for it. In a sense this suits us well enough. But sin too is a kind of witness. We can say what we like but our approach to life, the way we live, is a statement to those around us about what we really believe, what we live for, and what, if anything, we are prepared to die for. The Christian witness, the author of Hebrews suggests, will focus on Jesus, take courage from his example and persevere in the fight against sin to the point of death.

The Christian martyr, in imitation of Jesus, offers his life's blood in witness to the truth. The rest of us are called to something more modest - but perhaps no less difficult. Every time we give up one of our little sins we face a minor death. And every time we accept the grace of a fresh conversion we die a very real death. For to throw off everything that hinders us, especially the sin that clings so easily, and keep running in the race we have started, is to die to our past, who we have been as sinners, with all its attachments and entanglements and hasten to meet God, with courage and determination, in all the events and circumstances of our lives as they unfold and develop before us.

That would be witness enough for most of us, a source of consternation to those who would prefer us to stay the way we are, a little flame in the great fire of the Spirit that Jesus came to set ablaze upon the earth and that brings, in the end, a peace the world cannot give.

*Jeremiah 38:4-6.8-10 / Hebrews 12:1-4 / Luke 12:48-53*

## *Twenty-First Sunday*

*Someone said to him: Sir, will there be only a few saved?*

It is a question any of us might ask, brothers and sisters in Christ, if we have been listening to the Sunday gospels over these last few weeks and have felt the weight of the demands Jesus makes of his disciples and become all the more conscious of our own weakness.

Today we hear Jesus say: Try to enter by the narrow door, because, I tell you, many will try to enter and will not succeed. The narrow door, he is saying, is still open for the present but if we delay our attempt to enter we may leave it too late and find the door locked against us. We may have come to take for granted our place at the feast in the kingdom of God and then be unpleasantly surprised to find ourselves excluded and others let in that we might have thought unlikely candidates for sal-vation: Yes, there are those now last who will be first, and those now first who will be last.

We need to be shaken out of a false sense of security which says to us something like: If God is so good and heaven so spacious surely we will all be saved in the end and I can have nothing to worry about. We need to avoid too the discouragement which says: If not many are saved, what chance do I have? So why bother?

The point is that the door is narrow and entrance not easily gained. It is about our struggle for reality in the circumstances of our daily lives. It is about our search for our own personal truth, our search for God. In the end it is about our suffering: all the suffering that life brings us, all the suffering that we bring upon ourselves. We are confronted by the seriousness of life. We believe, as Hebrews reminds us, that we are God's children, that all our suffering has meaning, for it is somehow, in ways that we may never understand, part of our training. And we sense, that if properly used, it can bear fruit in peace and goodness.

We do not pretend that suffering cannot paralyse and destroy the lives it touches but at a deeper level we know for ourselves that it can take us to the heart of who we are, the heart of our own personal reality, and that in our struggle to understand we begin to grow and flourish in ways we could never have anticipated. We learn a new kindness, a new gentleness, a new compassion. We begin to realise that it is above all our suffering that has shaped us and made us who we are. We begin to suspect that if real peace and real goodness are to be possible for us we need to allow God to train us for them as best he can, as parents train their children to prepare them for life, sometimes to good effect, sometimes less so.

Try your best to enter by the narrow door, Jesus urges us. He means the narrow door of reality that leads to life, the door that opens from the cross into resurrection, where our

search for God is rewarded and our
personal truth comes to meet us.

So hold up your limp arms and
steady your trembling knees and
smooth out the path you tread.

*Isaiah 66:18-21 / Hebrews 12:5-7.11.13 /
Luke 13:22-30*

## *Twenty-Second Sunday*

*The heart of a sensible man will reflect on parables, an attentive ear is the sage's dream.*

When we reflect on today's parable, brothers and sisters in Christ, we no doubt recall one or other of our own moments of social embarrassment. Our self-importance was dented and we feel the pain of it still. Unless, that is, we have learnt humility in the meantime. For humility is the death of pride and pride is certainly one source of much unnecessary pain in human life. We suffer for our pride and we make others suffer for it too.

There is no cure for the proud man's malady, we heard in the Old Testament reading, since an evil growth has taken root in him. Jesus does indeed recognise the problem but suggests that there is a remedy: Everyone who exalts himself will be humbled - yes, indeed - but the man who humbles himself will be exalted. For the Christian disciple the life and death of Jesus are the example and pattern of his own humility.

Humility is quite simply truth. To be humble is to walk in truth on a road that leads to freedom. To be proud is to create one's own prison in a private world of fantasy and illusion. Everyone who exalts himself will be humbled: that is the inevitable pain of living a lie. The man who humbles himself will be exalted: there is pain too of course in moving out of personal darkness into the light of truth. The difference is that we freely choose such pain confident that it will be worth it.

But that is not a choice we can make on our own. In human terms there is indeed no cure for the proud man's malady, an evil growth has taken root in him. We choose the path of humility at the appointed moment when grace strikes. Until grace comes, we may well see the wisdom of humility but it is beyond our reach. There will be moments when the proud envy the humble, for often the humble receive as a gift from life much that the proud have striven hard to achieve. But humility itself is not an achievement. It comes from not trying too hard. If we are too proud of our humility it does not work at all.

And humility carries us far beyond what pride might have thought possible. If at first Jesus seems only to be giving his fellow-guests a little hint about how they might avoid social embarrassment in his next breath he turns to their host with a sweeping suggestion about whom he should invite to his parties. The fact that two thousand years of Christianity have changed so little of all that must be the greatest embarrassment of all.

*Ecclesiasticus 3:17-20.28-29 / Hebrews 12:18-19.22-24 / Luke 14:1.7-14*

## *Twenty-Third Sunday*

*Lord, make us know the shortness of our life that we may gain wisdom of heart.*

Wisdom, brothers and sisters in Christ, is a gift of the Holy Spirit that enables us to see ourselves and our world with the eyes of God. Wisdom shows us how to face reality and make the best of it. And it is in our struggle for reality against the encroachments of fantasy and illusion that we discover the wisdom of the cross of Christ and come to share in his victory over the follies of the human world as it passes away.

Anyone who does not carry his cross and come after me, says Jesus, cannot be my disciple. This will mean different things to us at different stages of our journey. Sometimes it won't mean very much or anything at all. Sometimes we will resent its implications. But in the end it is our only hope, the Christian key to the meaning of our lives.

Perhaps we think of this or that affliction as our cross and put up with it as best we can. But is that wisdom or just resignation? And surely it is inappropriate and indeed insensitive to refer to all the tragic things that happen in people's lives as crosses to be borne with patience and humility. The wisdom of the cross is much larger than that. The cross that Jesus invites us to carry as the hope of our future is the whole burden of our past and the limitations of our present. And indeed, which of you here, intending to build a tower, would not first sit down and work out the cost to see if he had enough to complete it? Life creates unrealistic expectations that cannot be fulfilled. Wisdom teaches us to live within our limitations. It is a painful lesson, this crucifixion of our expectations that is the price of real life.

If anyone comes to me without hating his father, mother, wife, children, brothers, sisters, yes and his own life too, he cannot be my disciple. This bewildering text offers a more fundamental version of the same painful lesson. It is about battling against the illusions that cut us off from reality and from one another. The price of real life is the surrender of the illusions we have grown comfortable with. Do we never notice how much we hate the real people we collide with in daily life because we are in love with the fantasies we have woven around them?

We have expectations about the people we say we love, mother and father, husband or wife, sons and daughters, our families and our friends. And how our expectations make them suffer. We all suffer the pain of other people's expectations and our own. Until I come to hate my expectations of the people in my life I cannot begin to love, for the essence of love is acceptance and not expectation. But our expectations are dear to us above all else and to hate them is to crucify our most deeply rooted fantasies. For as long as we cling to our illusions we cannot be disciples of Jesus.

If we refuse our cross we are left with only this epitaph: here lies someone who started to build and was unable to finish. It is the epitaph of someone who never lived at all, just another victim of fantasy and illusion.

To carry our cross is to surrender our extravagant expectations and begin to live within the solid reality of our limitations. Lord, make us know the shortness of our life that we may gain wisdom of heart. Amen.

*Wisdom 9:13-18 / Philemon 9-10.12-17 / Luke 14:25-33*

## *Twenty-Fourth Sunday*

*The Pharisees and the scribes complained.*

The Pharisees and the scribes complained, brothers and sisters in Christ, because that is what Pharisees and scribes do. They complain. This man, they said, welcomes sinners and eats with them. That was their complaint about Jesus, their complaint about what might well seem his whole attractiveness, indeed the clearest expression of his divinity, his concern for the lost sheep, his quest for the lost drachma. They had missed the point, as Pharisees and scribes so often do. It was the sinners they so despised that understood what Jesus was about and sought his company and wanted to hear what he had to say.

What makes a sinner? We all have our own ideas about that. Sinners are, generally speaking, other people. We do have our own sins now and again but somehow the notion that we are sinners in need of salvation is just too big to grapple with. And that is the problem of the Pharisees and scribes. They keep most of the rules most of the time. If anyone is in God's good books, they are. And here is Jesus appealing to a different constituency and hinting at different rules. Jesus may very well have come into the world to save sinners but he should surely start by congratulating those who keep the rules - just to make it clear whose side he's on. Instead here he is welcoming sinners and eating with them. If this man had an ounce of religious sophistication, they smirk, he would see what sort of people he has running after him.

The message of Jesus is that God loves sinners. That's something the Pharisees and scribes resent. They are desperate to tone down that message and explain it away. For them God's proper business is to punish sinners. He can't possibly be allowed to love them until they repent and conform. Pharisees and scribes create their own God in their own image and likeness.

The God and Father of Our Lord Jesus Christ does not punish sinners. He knows that sin is its own punishment. He sent his Son into the world to save sinners, for he loves them, he cares about them, it concerns him what becomes of them. No one is excluded from his love.

And so Jesus makes a special effort to reach out to the Pharisees and the scribes - because they are a special kind of sinner, the most difficult kind, victims of bad religion. And in reaching out to them he reaches out to the Pharisee lurking in the heart of each one of us, the scribe nagging away in the pit of our mind. The God of Jesus is a surprise, unutterably different from anything we have been led to expect.

In reality, each one of us is that lost sheep. Each one of us is that lost drachma. God loves us. He cares about us. It concerns him what becomes of us. And if our religion leads us to judge others and despise them then our first inkling that there is something wrong with our religion will bring a tremor of joy to the heart of God and a beginning of rejoicing among his angels.

*Exodus 32:7-11.13-14 / First Timothy 1:12-17 / Luke 15:1-32*

## *Twenty-Fifth Sunday*

*No servant can be the slave of two masters....*
*You cannot be the slave both of God and of money.*

Money, brothers and sisters in Christ, is a word that strikes a false note when dropped into the sort of spiritual reflection we expect in a Sunday homily. It is a word we would rather not hear in church. And that is very interesting - because the mention of money strikes a very deep chord indeed within each one of us. Yes, we would like to dismiss that chord as a jumble of false notes but in fact it resonates through our whole being with an unpleasant sound. It stirs up obscure emotions and impassioned reactions, for the mere mention of money touches very sensitive parts of our personalities. If ever we allowed the thought of money to invade our examination of conscience we would find that we had a lot to talk about in confession. If we lift the lid on this dangerous area we are confronted with our deepest fears and desires, our greed and our avarice, our most powerful feelings of guilt, envy and resentment.

And there we catch a salutary glimpse of what Jesus means when he warns us that we cannot be the slave of both God and money. No servant can be the slave of two masters. And that is why when we hear the word spoken in a religious context we are immediately uneasy. Jesus is not simply asking us to be wary of money and what it might do to us. He is begging us to recognize how deeply we are already ensnared. And this is not about how much money we have, or how little. It is about how important the money obsession is in our lives, in our hearts and in our heads. How it controls our thoughts and our feelings and our actions.

Those who have more money than they need have, of course, opport-unities to do a great deal of good in the world, provided their own needs are not too extravagant. And those who really do not have enough for their basic needs carry a cruel burden that is a challenge and an opportunity for those who can help. But for all of us money remains a powerful symbol of our slavery because it expresses our preoccupation with tomorrow, our deeply-rooted fear of not having enough in some future crisis.

Our fear of not having enough, our fear about our own personal survival, is what distorts our lives and leads us into sin. It is why we are sinners in the first place. It is no small thing to say that Jesus has ransomed us. He has ransomed us from all that slavery that money symbolises. For to be a slave of God is to be the slave of no one, free of all such entanglements, a free man, a free woman living without fear in the present moment. It is the alternative lifestyle in a world where money can buy almost everything else.

The children of this world are more astute in dealing with their own kind than are the children of light. We could all learn something from them.

*Amos 8:4-7 / First Timothy 2:1-6 / Luke 16:1-13*

## *Twenty-Sixth Sunday*

*The rich man also died and was buried.*

Death puts things in perspective, brothers and sisters in Christ. A long spiritual tradition teaches us that the daily remembrance of death can enrich and transform our lives. Death is the only certainty in life. We are the poorer for forgetting it. When we do remember we see through the web of silliness in which we are enmeshed and catch a glimpse of what is really important. The theory is that when we know that we are only passing through we become kinder to ourselves and to others. We treat others more compassionately, with more patience, with more tolerance, when we look at them and see the skeleton through the skin. And this spiritual focusing on death is not at all morbid and is not meant to be. It is in fact the only genuine path to a true enjoyment of life here and now.

Jesus' story about Lazarus shocks us and unsettles us in different ways. We might well recognise something of ourselves in both protagonists for we all have our own wealth and we all have our own poverty. The rich man in the story is not blamed for anything in particular. It is his indifference that is so damning. Nor is Lazarus praised for anything he has done but his name means "God helps" and that is the clue to his ultimate salvation. Perhaps the rich man thought "God helps those who help themselves". Perhaps when he saw Lazarus lying at his gate he gave thanks to God for his own wealth and well-being. It is only our poverty, no matter how wealthy we are, that teaches us that God helps, for God helps only when there is no other help. This is what Lazarus knew when the dogs came and licked his sores. It is in the crises of our lives where we can neither help ourselves nor receive help from others that God comes to meet us.

God helps. But death is the defining moment. We become what we have been and are and will be forever. Jesus portrays the rich man as pained that this message was never put forcefully enough to him in life. He would have Lazarus sent back to warn his brothers so that they at least might escape his desperate fate. They have Moses and the prophets, he is told, let them listen to them. We too have Moses and the prophets, or rather we have all the Scriptures and the Church, we have the experience of the religion we encountered as children, at home and at school, and our experience of what that religion means to us now, whatever it does mean to us now, in our everyday lives. All that speaks to us and solicits our conversion - or impedes it, as the case may be.

No, Lazarus is not going to come back from the grave to convince us about God or anything else. But perhaps there are other Lazarus people lying at our gates as we enjoy the illusion of our wealth and the magnificent feasting of the fantasy that we have all we need and the foolish notion that we are all we ought to be. God's hope for us is that one day we will trip over one of these Lazarus people as we rush about in our frenzy of indifference and that the fall will open our eyes to our own need of him, the God who helps only when we are beyond help. Yes, the prospect of death wonderfully concentrates the mind, teaching us our need for God and making us alive as never before.

*Amos 6:1.4-7 / First Timothy 6:11-16 / Luke 16:19-31*

## *Twenty-Seventh Sunday*

*When you have done all you have
been told to do, say: We are merely
servants. We have done no more than
our duty.*

Somehow, brothers and sisters in
Christ, we all like to be given credit
for what we have done. Perhaps we
have achieved something. Perhaps
we have been generous. Perhaps we
have shown forgiveness when it
might not have been expected. We
like to be acknowledged, recognized,
rewarded. Today's gospel challenges
this very human need. Must the
master really be grateful to the
servant for doing what he was told?
We are merely servants: we have
done no more than our duty. When
we do something that is right and
good and appropriate we are to pass
on without waiting for the applause.
We are simply to thank God for as
often as we do the right thing it is a
sign that his grace is at work within
us.

When we go wrong, when we do
things we are ashamed of, when we

hurt others, we realise that we are on our own. We have only ourselves to blame. God is no longer with us. Not indeed that he has abandoned us. We have abandoned him. We have gone our own way. We have refused the guidance of grace and we cannot evade the consequences of that. The pain we feel when that happens, the pain of not being right with ourselves because we are not right with God, is itself a grace because it can be the beginning of a return to grace, a return to God. It is God's way of inviting us back.

The pain of being separated from God can of course take us in the wrong direction. It can become so severe that it drives us to distraction and into the spiral of addiction that our environment offers the bored, the lonely and the bewildered. This would seem to be the very opposite of grace and yet within the very degradation of sin grace is lurking and waiting to strike. Falling into the gutter is a chance to see the sky, to look up at the stars, perhaps for the first time. Grace is lurking in our self-inflicted darkness, waiting to strike. In the end the burden of sin, our weariness of heart, the dreary dullness of our everyday lives can bring us to our knees before the cross of Christ our Saviour and in the that awesome silence where we know ourselves even as we are known we will hear the invitation to return. Perhaps we will accept the gift of resurrection there and then. Such is the miracle of grace. Or perhaps we will need to follow a longer path, a path of penance and detachment, leading us into a fuller knowledge of who we are and what we are called to.

But, however short or long the journey, when grace does strike at last we are suddenly alive. And we have a good laugh at the meticulous account we have kept of all that we do for God and for one another.

*Habakkuk 1:2-3; 2:2-4 / Second Timothy 1:6-8.13-14 / Luke 17:5-10*

## *Twenty-Eighth Sunday*

*Jesus! Master! Take pity on us.*

The incident in today's gospel is an odd one, brothers and sisters in Christ. Nowhere else do we have an account of Jesus curing a whole group of people. Here ten lepers come to meet him, together in a group. The well-known physical symptoms and the early death are not perhaps the most distressing aspects of leprosy. Worst of all is the exclusion of the leper from ordinary life. And so leprosy is a potent symbol of all those things that exclude us from the ordinary. Ten lepers - but they were not always lepers. Before the disease struck they were just ordinary people like any of us. But now they are lepers and in their exclusion they find solidarity with one another: their leprosy brings them together.

They stood some way off and called to him: Jesus! Master! Take pity on us. It is a prayer. And Jesus simply tells them: Go and show yourselves to the priests. This was the Jewish law: those who were cured of their leprosy were to have their cure verified so that they could be re-admitted to ordinary life.

This might have been the end of the incident but then something un-expected happened that seemed to take Jesus by surprise. Finding himself cured, one of them turned back praising God at the top of his voice and threw himself at the feet of Jesus and thanked him. This man was not only a leper, he was also a Samaritan and so doubly excluded, doubly marginalized. Were not all ten made clean? The other nine, where are they? We do not know. We do not know what became of them afterwards. They went back to their ordinary lives, their families, their work, their amusements and they disappeared. After a while they even forgot that they had ever been lepers.

Not so the Samaritan. Finding himself cured, he turned back praising God at the top of his voice. He threw himself at the feet of Jesus and thanked him. He knew that in

Jesus he had met God. And so today's gospel is after all about one man and how he met Jesus and accepted salvation. Stand up, Jesus told him, and go on your way. Your faith has saved you. The other nine were merely cured of their leprosy and disappeared back into the camouflage of ordinary living. The Samaritan met Jesus. He was saved by his faith. He had emerged from the ordinary, somehow subtly different. Indeed we sense that he was never quite the same ever again.

And we remember, perhaps uneasily, that the selfsame thing could happen to anyone of us when we place ourselves honestly in the presence of Jesus.

*Second Kings 5:14-17 / Second Timothy 2:8-13 Luke 17:11-19*

## *Twenty-Ninth Sunday*

*But when the Son of Man comes, will he find any faith on earth?*

One of the most important things Christians are said to believe about Jesus, brothers and sisters in Christ, is that he will come again. Indeed you might say that a Christian is precisely that, a person who is waiting for Jesus to come again, expecting him, passionately, at every moment. So what if Jesus did actually come today, this minute, to this place? Would he find any faith in this church? Can we take that risk? The risk of allowing his question to become our question too? When the Son of Man comes, will he find any faith among us here?

Is God an obvious presence in our lives and the lives of the people around us? Or have we long ago stopped praying and completely lost heart? Certainly we struggle at times with the weakness of our own belief, our unbelief, our lack of faith. And are we not sometimes tempted to wonder about the people around us:

do they believe very much or anything at all? Can we really believe that they believe? Perhaps they believe that they believe but are quite mistaken.

Jesus told his disciples this parable about the need to pray continually and never lose heart. The widow, we can imagine, is a strong personality. She does not take "No" for an answer. She comes back again and again demanding justice until she is vindicated. The judge too is of robust character and not untypical of those who enjoy exercising arbitrary authority over others. But we should not take him to stand for God in the story. He is simply there to provide a structure for the parable.

We make an enormous mistake when we think of God as an instance we can usefully bully, pester and worry to death until he gives us what we want. To think of that kind of thing as prayer is an appalling sacrilege. God is not mocked. Too often when we demand justice we are really only looking for vengeance. We need to be more honest with ourselves about that. Justice is not served at all when all that is delivered is revenge.

The lesson of the widow's passionate demand for her just rights in this parable is that we are to pray continually and never lose heart until at last God's kingdom comes and God's justice and peace become reality for all humanity. God will see justice done in our world when we learn to cry out to him in prayer day and night. Not the impertinent prayer that tells God what to do but the prayer that Jesus teaches us: Thy kingdom come. Thy will be done on earth as it is done in heaven. True prayer brings us closer and closer to God until our heart is in tune with his heart and we are at peace.

Do we believe this passionately enough for it to come to pass in our time, in our lives? When the Son of Man comes will he find any faith on earth? If Jesus were to come here today would he find his kingdom in us and among us? Or have we simply forgotten that we are supposed to waiting for him to come again? Have

we given up praying altogether and
lost heart once and for all?

*Exodus 17:8-13 / Second Timothy 3:14 – 4:2
/ Luke 18:1-8*

## *Thirtieth Sunday*

*He stood some distance away, not daring even to raise his eyes to heaven; but he beat his breast and said: God, be merciful to me, a sinner.*

The parable in today's gospel, brothers and sisters in Christ, suggests that there is a right way of praying and a wrong way of praying. But it is not quite as simple as that. Those who pride themselves on being virtuous and despise everyone else will imagine that Jesus is addressing the typical Pharisee concern about how to deal with God. The Pharisee in every generation wants to know, and as precisely as possible, how to deal with God.

And so the Pharisee who has heard this parable will continue in his heart to be grateful that he is not like the rest of humanity, he will continue to fast twice a week, he will continue to pay tithes on all he gets and, in addition, in future when he goes to the Temple to pray he will keep his distance, he will keep his eyes fixed firmly on the ground, he will beat his breast and he will be heard repeating in a loud whisper: God, be merciful to me, a sinner.

That is the whole tragedy of the Pharisee - it is so important to him to be seen and heard - especially to be seen and heard doing and saying the right things - that he continues to miss the point of Jesus' teaching about prayer. The tragedy of the Pharisee is that getting the words and gestures right without a radical change of heart is simply a grotesque hypocrisy. There is something naïvely honest about his original prayer: I thank you, God, that I am not grasping, unjust, adulterous like the rest of mankind, and particularly that I am not like this tax collector here. We almost feel embarrassed for him. He evokes our sympathy. We know that he will never get right with God without a radical change of heart.

When we pray it is right and good that we should thank God for all the times that we have been enabled by his grace to say no to sin. But there is no virtue in making a list of all the sins we haven't committed. There is no virtue in avoiding all kinds of sins that we have no inclination or opportunity to commit. Even if we could say that we keep nine and three-quarters of the ten command-ments, so what? Unless by such a process of elimination we come closer to identifying what it is that separates us from God, for separated from God we certainly are.

Two elements are missing in the Pharisee's prayer and they are closely related: a sense of his own need for God's forgiveness and a sense of compassion for other sinners. Be-cause he is so enchanted by all the evil that he hasn't done he fails to come to terms with his own sinful-ness, he fails to ask God to forgive him his sins. And because he has no sense of his own sinfulness he despises the more obvious sinners around him. Forgive us our tres-passes as we forgive those who trespass against us - part of the prayer that Jesus taught us that is not at all easy for the Pharisee lurking in the heart of each one of us.

Real prayer goes beyond words and gestures to the truth about life. Real prayer is about listening to God. Real prayer is the end of pride and the beginning of humility. God, be merciful to me, a sinner. If we could make that prayer our own it would become a song that fills our hearts with the warmth of God's forgiveness and opens our eyes to the God waiting to be set free in our fellow sinners.

*Ecclesiasticus 35:12-14.16-19 / Second Timothy 4:6-8.16-18 / Luke 18:9-14*

## Thirty-First Sunday

*They all complained when they saw what was happening. He has gone to stay at a sinner's house, they said.*

We don't perhaps realise how foolish we are left looking, brothers and sisters in Christ, when we fail to see things from God's point of view. But there are in fact two sides to every story. There is the way things look and the way things are. Everything has an inside as well as an outside. Our mistake is to take appearance for reality.

Look at Zacchaeus. From the outside he appears a wealthy man, a man to be reckoned with. And yet today's Gospel story is about a familiar and fundamental religious theme: the strange poverty of the rich. The materially advantaged among us do not necessarily tremble when they hear that it is easier for a camel to pass through the eye of a needle and so on because very often they have a keener experience of the poverty of every human being before God. And to be spiritually poor is, paradoxically, to be ripe for conversion. Zacchaeus is a conversion just waiting to happen. All it takes is a brief encounter with Jesus.

Jesus understands this strange poverty of the rich. The crowd does not. They all complained when they saw what was happening. We can hear the venom in their words: He has gone to stay at a sinner's house. Some of the self-righteous will long be too immature for conversion. Others have simply gone stale. But God exercises an inventive indulgence with them all.

It's safe in the crowd, of course. But those who play safe have only death to look forward to and somehow Zacchaeus knew it. He wanted to see what kind of man Jesus was, but he was too short and could not see him for the crowd. So he ran ahead and climbed a tree. Rather indecorous for someone like Zacchaeus to be seen running in the street. And climbing a tree! How often have you exposed yourself to such ridicule in your efforts to catch a glimpse of Jesus? But such efforts are rewarded:

Zacchaeus come down. Hurry, because I must stay at your house today.

It is no cheap joy, this joy of conversion. And in more ways than one: Zacchaeus is going to give half his property to the poor, and if he has cheated anybody he will pay them back four times the amount.

Today salvation has come to this house, says Jesus. Not today, thank you - is our usual response. But Jesus has come to seek out and save what was lost and so whether we like it or not he will continue to threaten each one of us with his unwelcome joy.

*Wisdom 11:22 – 12:2 / Second Thessalonians 1:11 – 2:2 / Luke 19:1-10*

## *Thirty-Second Sunday*

*I shall see your face and be filled, when I awake, with the sight of your glory.*

The Sadducees we meet in today's gospel, brothers and sisters in Christ, do not share the conviction of the seven Maccabee brothers that the King of the world will raise them up after their courageous death. The Sadducees represent a different and indeed, within Judaism, a more traditional view. For them death is the end of the individual and his consciousness. God's blessing is shown rather in the survival of their children and their children's children and the ongoing prosperity of their clan. They refuse to believe in anything they cannot see with their own eyes and touch with their own hands. Sadducee conviction focuses sharply, and exclusively, on the world of here and now, on personal achievement and material success.

We can understand their concern then about dying without leaving anyone to carry on their fame and fortune. They are glad to have it in writing from Moses that it is the duty of an unmarried man to marry his dead brother's widow in order to provide heirs for him. And, so sure are they that death is the end, they use this Jewish law to poke fun at those who believe in the resurrection of the dead: suppose there were seven brothers and they all died childless whose wife would the widow be when they all rose again?

Whatever we may feel about their argument, we readily recognise the polemical tone, the unpleasantness of such hyper-conviction, the scorn for any alternative view. But there is a serious point, for we all have our own questions about what has become of the members of our own families and other friends who have died and indeed about what we can expect when it is our turn to die. What is it like for them? What will it be like for us?

We are Easter people. We believe that Jesus rose from the dead never to die again. We believe that if we die with him we shall also live with

112

him. That is the promise of our Baptism and it is renewed and refreshed every time we share his Body and Blood in the Mass. We are committed to dying more and more to sin everyday so that we may be fully alive to God already now in this life and forever in the world to come.

Our speculation about that world to come does not take us very far - and it is perhaps best to admit as much. It is another dimension of reality beyond anything we can grasp with our senses. For those who have known the joy and fulfilment of marriage it is not perhaps a great advertisement for heaven to be reminded that marriage ends with death. The marriage vows go that far and no further - as long as we both shall live, till death us do part. But it must be that the joy and fulfilment of which a good marriage is a foretaste in this life is the very substance of heaven for it is love that gives us our first inkling that we human beings have something of God in us and that he cannot mean us to die into eternal nothingness.

That is why we give thanks to God our Father in our Masses for the Dead that in Jesus our Saviour the hope of blessed resurrection has dawned so that those saddened by the certainty of dying might be consoled by the promise of immortality to come. For God's faithful people life is changed not ended and when our earthly dwelling turns to dust an eternal dwelling is made ready for us in heaven where we will sing his glory with the angels and saints for all eternity. Amen.

*Second Maccabees 7:1-2.9-14 / Second Thessalonians 2:16 – 3:5 / Luke 20:27-38*

Printed in Great Britain
by Amazon